Vietnam

A Vietnam Travel Guide Written By A Vietnamese.

The Best Travel Tips By a Local.

1

D1444153

Table of Contents

About Our Guides - Why They Are Unique

We were travelers really tired of the typical boring travel guides. In most cases, wikipedia is much better, complete and dynamic. When we traveled, we tried to ask friends, or friends of friends who were "locals". That is where we got the best tips by far, the most valuable ones about our travel destinations.

This guide tries to do the same as the "ask a local", but it is (maybe!) better organized and more complete. In all our guides, we hire a "local" writer, and then we edit to be sure that the guide is complete, unique, fun and interesting. Typically we won't add too many maps or photos, since you can have all that on the internet and we like to give you only unique and original content that you won't find easily.

Since we use different writers for each city, you will see (after you fall in love with our guides and download more than one), that they are not standardized. Each city is different, each "local" is different, and each guide is different. And we really like that.

Thanks for being here and we really hope that you like it. Enjoy!

Chapter 1: History Of Vietnam

The term Vietnam comes from an old term Nam Viet which literally translates to Southern Viet. This term was eventually adopted by Emperor Gia Long in 1802 and made Vietnam as the official name of the country. Vietnam is a long yet narrow strip of land that lies east of the Indochina peninsula. It is bordered by China to the north, Laos and Cambodia to the west, Gulf of Thailand to the South, and South China Sea to the East. Its strategic location has led to quite a number of colonial encounters which contributed to the very colourful and vibrant culture that is unique to Vietnam. Contrary to the colourful and lively culture practiced currently, Vietnam has undergone such gruesome undertakings against its conquerors in the past which took a toll in the country's economic development and freedom. Up until now, travellers can easily find traces of Vietnam's dark past in some of its scenic, tourist areas.

Chinese Colonization

200 BC to the early 16th century, Vietnam has struggled independence from its constant colonizer, China. Being land-locked with one of the strongest empires of the ancient times, Vietnam had a difficult time regaining freedom from several Chinese dynasties. The first successful attempt to colonize Vietnam happened in 207 BC when a Chinese general by the name of Zhao Tuo overthrew the first known Vietnamese state, the An Duong Vuong. This Chinese rule took over Vietnam for more than a century until 938 AD when a Vietnamese lord named Ngo Quyen finally won over the Chinese rulers and regained full freedom from the very long Chinese regime. This was the time when the Buddhist religion gained popularity in the region and the name Dai Viet was used to call what was then Vietnam.

For the third time in early 13th century, the Chinese once again successfully took over Vietnam. This time the Chinese Ming dynasty ruled over Vietnam for more than a year. This regime was cut short by the courageous act of Le Loi, who brought freedom back to

Vietnam. It was during this time that Vietnam started expanding southwards, conquering a part of the Khmer region and the Champa Kingdom.

For the fourth and final time, the Chinese attempted to conquer Vietnam however the strength of the Le dynasty that was founded by Le Loi was far too strong to overthrow that is why independence prevailed in Vietnam. This strength even expanded the reign of Vietnam to the West which covered a part of the Mekong River and the Central Highlands.

French Colonization

In the mid-1800s, the independence savoured by the Vietnamese for more than 2,000 years was interrupted by the French colonizers. The French forces slowly conquered Vietnam from the south until it was able to take over the entire region. In 1887, Vietnam became a part of the French IndoChina Union. A handful of changes and modernization occurred during the French regime – modern system of education, modern architecture, modern religion of Catholicism, and modern culture. Most of the French inhabitants stayed in Saigon or more known presently as Ho Chi Minh. This is where the French introduced new agricultural crops such as tobacco, coffee, tea, and indigo. Despite the progress brought about by the French regime, the Vietnamese still called for independence and self-governance. This cry was oftentimes neglected by the French. For this reason, a number of Vietnamese patriots surfaced like Emperor Ho Chi Minh who tried to overthrow the French rule; unfortunately this was not realized instead the French presence became even more powerful in the 1940's.

During the Second World War, the Japanese took over Vietnam and became a station for Japanese troops and artilleries. This period became one of Vietnam's darkest periods because the Japanese exploited the natural resources of the region which eventually led to the Famine of 1945. This event has awoken patriotic hearts and this led to the First Indochina War between Ho Chi Minh's troops called Viet Minh and French troops. The Viet Minh was able to slowly succeed its way to the north of Vietnam and was able to take over Hanoi as well. Because of this successful take over, the French rule over Vietnam was dissolved and Vietnam was divided into two political regions – North Vietnam which was ruled by Ho Chi Minh and the South Vietnam which was ruled by Bao Dai. What was supposed to be a smooth transition to unify the two existing states became another gruesome event because Bao Dai was overthrown by his politically greedy brother Ngo Dinh Nhu and announced himself as the president of the Republic of Vietnam.

Vietnam War

The declaration of Ngo Dinh Nhu as the president of the Republic of Vietnam sparked tensions between the North and the South Vietnamese rulers. The tension even grew stronger when the North Vietnam rulers allied with the Soviet Union while South Vietnam was aided by the Americans. The war lasted for almost 10 years and only ceased in 1973 due to the Paris Peace Accords which ordered all American troops to vacate

Vietnam. In 1976, the North and South Vietnam were joined together to form the Socialist Republic of Vietnam. The war killed millions of citizens and damaged most of the country's prime structures.

Present Day Government

Vietnam is one of the 5 countries around the world that still follows a communist type of government. The Socialist Republic of Vietnam is led by two influential positions – President as the head of state and Prime Minister as the head of government. Both the President and the Prime Minister head the executive branch of the government while the National Assembly of Vietnam heads the legislative branch. The National Assembly is composed of 500 members each of whom has a 4-year term. The third branch of government is the judicial branch dictated by the Constitution of Vietnam.

Chapter 2 : Geography And Climate

The shape of Vietnam can be compared to a crooked hourglass where it is wide at the northern and southern tips, while it tapers at the center. It is a long and narrow land that stretches for 1,000 miles from the northern tip to the southern end, but only stretches for 31 miles from west to east. Its coastline is twice as long as its distance from north to south, which makes Vietnam a fishing as well as farming community. The shape of Vietnam can also be compared to a bamboo pole with rice baskets at either ends.

Northern Vietnam

The northern region of Vietnam is made fertile by the Red River delta. This river created a swampy region in the northern lowlands of Vietnam and a swampy forest at the northern-central region. Aside from a swampy region in the north, there is an abundance of limestone formation making the northern region rich in mineral deposits. Along its coastal region, the land experiences the tropical climate however, unlike the southern region, the rainy season in Hanoi and Vinh peaks towards the end of the year. September and October are the months that receive most amount of rainfall but there is still a generous amount of precipitation until January.

Central Highlands

The Central Highlands of Vietnam covers the region of Tay Nguyen, which is bordered by Laos and Cambodia. It is called a highland because the population living in this region is situated on top of interconnecting plateaus, the Kong Plong Plateau, the Pleiku Plateau, the Kong Ha Nung Plateau, the Mdrak Plateau, the Mo Nong Plateau, the Dak Lak Plateau, the Lam Vien Plateau, and the Di Linh Plateau. These plateaus offer a very good view of the mountain ranges found in the Central Highlands. All the provinces covered by this region have relatively cooler temperatures because of its altitude.

Southern Vietnam

The Southern Vietnam region starts from Da Nang all the way down to Ho Chi Minh City. The general topography of this region composes of lowlands that are dry and arid. The southern region of Vietnam is dry because of the effects of the plateaus in the Central Highlands which restricts the flow of wet air to the south.

The Southern part of Vietnam is also greatly composed of a stretch of coastal lands. The land in this region is also bordered by the great Mekong River that is responsible for fertilizing the agricultural lands and also giving the inhabitants a main avenue for transportation and even commerce.

The general climate in the south is warm and humid. The region experiences a lot of rainfall throughout the year; however rain is concentrated during the months of July to September. This region is slightly warmer and a lot drier than the north.

Chapter 3: Culture And Religion

The culture of Vietnam has been heavily influenced by the Ancient Chinese civilization. According to historical artifacts, Northern Vietnam has one of the oldest civilizations found in Asia and this civilization has been in constant connection with the Chinese. When Northern Vietnam gained independence from China, its civilization started sprawling southwards where it was introduced to a new community, the Khmers. In time, the French colonies came and this also left a huge impact on the culture of Vietnam. That is why when you go around Vietnam, you will see a lot of French inspired architecture, French inspired cuisine and many more.

As it is greatly shaped by the Chinese civilization, the religions practiced in Vietnam also originated in the Eastern part of Asia. The early religions followed here are Buddhism, Taoism, and Confucianism. With the arrival of the French, the country was introduced to Christianity and Catholicism. Finally, with the interaction with other races, Hinduism, Judaism, and Islam became part of the country's list of practiced religions. There are also countless of indigenous religions practiced throughout the country like Cao Dai. Out of all these religions, the religion with the most followers is Buddhism more particularly the three religion called Tam Giao. Tam Giao follows the three teachings of Tao, Confucius, and Buddha.

Chapter 4 : Getting to Vietnam

It is very easy to get to the major cities of Vietnam. The country can be accessed from any point in the globe.

By air

If you are coming from any other continent except for Asia, you might not find a straight flight to Vietnam. Do not let this stop you from traveling to this great place. It is actually very easy and cheap to find a connecting flight to Saigon or Hanoi.

Flights from North/South America:

There are a handful of international airlines that fly (with one stop) to Hanoi or Ho Chi Minh City from the East and West Coasts from United States. From the JFK Airport in New York, you can fly via Cathay Pacific to Hong Kong and transfer from Hong Kong to Ho Chi Minh or Hanoi. The same goes with Korean Air where you will have a stop at Incheon and transfer from

Incheon to Ho Chi Minh or Hanoi. From the West Coast like Los Angeles or San Francisco, you can also take Cathay Pacific or Korean Airline and have similar routes and lay overs. From Canada, one of the better options is to take Air Canada or Cathay Pacific to get to Vietnam.

There are also a handful of international airlines that fly (with one stop) to Hanoi or Ho Chi Minh from South America. For example, if you are traveling from Buenos Aires, Argentina, you may take Qatar Airlines to Doha, Qatar and transfer from Qatar to Hanoi or Ho Chi Minh. Travel time may take more than 24 hours but the beautiful service of an airline such as Qatar may make the long haul easier.

Flights from Europe:

There are more direct flights available in key cities in Europe via the flag carrier Vietnam Airlines. Vietnam Airlines flies straight to Paris, London, and Frankfurt from Hanoi so if you want to go to Vietnam you can easily access it by going to Paris, London, or Frankfurt first. This is not the only option though. For example, if you are flying from Madrid, Spain and you want to get to Ho Chi Minh, you may take Etihad Airways or Emirates Airlines. For a pretty cheap airfare, you can fly to either Abu Dhabi or Dubai and transfer planes to get to Saigon. Other airlines that have similar routes coming from major cities in Europe are Air Berlin, KLM, Turkish Airlines, Alitalia, and British Airways.

Flights from Africa:

Vietnam is also easily accessible from Africa via some international airlines that offer a one-stop flight to either Ho Chi Minh or Saigon. For example, if you are flying from Johannesburg, South Africa to Saigon, you may take Singapore Airlines which offers the shortest flying time possible. Other major airlines that have similar flight plans are Etihad Airways, Emirates Airlines, South African Airlines, and even Vietnam Airlines.

Flights from Australia:

There are a lot of international airlines that fly to Vietnam with only one stop in between destinations. For example, if you are flying from Melbourne, you may take Air Asia or Qantas and have a quick stop in Kuala Lumpur or Singapore respectively before transferring to another plane that will take you to Hanoi or Ho Chi Minh.

Flights from Asia:

There are plenty of budget airlines that service directly to Hanoi or Ho Chi Minh. Companies such as Air Asia of Malaysia, Cebu Pacific of the Philippines, Tiger Air of Singapore, and many more can bring travellers to Vietnam for pretty low prices.

By land

Travellers going to Vietnam may reach it by land especially if they have been traversing the Indochina peninsula. You may just drive or take the bus to

Vietnam if you are coming from Laos or Cambodia or even Thailand. This could be a better alternative for backpackers who want to see and experience the terrain and the views of traveling from one country to another. Westerners should remember to fix their visas first prior to embarking on such a trip because this may delay your set schedule. If you are coming from Bangkok, Thailand and you plan to take a bus or train to Vietnam, it is best to arrange you visa before you even exit the airport. Processing your Vietnamese visa may take a couple of days and will definitely incur some expenses but you have to make sure that everything is ready before you cross borders. You may also need to process your Cambodian visa in advance because you will definitely pass by this country as well. The good news is you can process your Cambodian visa through the internet. You may access it via www.evisa.gov.kh.

It is also good to know that the roads leading to Vietnam are not as smooth and grand as the roads found in First World countries. Prepare for a bumpy and shaky ride that takes more than 24 hours. This is the usual travel route from Bangkok to Ho Chi Minh City: Bangkok to Siem Reap approximately 11 hours of travel, Siem Reap to Phnom Penh approximately 8 hours of travel, and Phnom Penh to Ho Chi Minh approximately 7 hours of travel.

Chapter 5: Hanoi, The Capital City

Declared as the capital of Vietnam in 1945, Hanoi is the second largest city in Vietnam. Its land area expands to 3,345km2 and its population as of 2014 is almost 7,100,000. Hanoi was declared as the country's capital after the end of the Vietnam War where the North Vietnamese faction outdid the South.

Geographic Location and Climate

Hanoi is situated at the Northern part of Vietnam and the city lies by the Red River Delta. Due to its unique location, this relatively humble area showcases three different topographic sceneries – the mountainous scenery, the midland scenery, and the delta scenery. As it is found near a mountainous region, Hanoi is situated at least 5 meters above sea level which makes its climate a little colder than the other parts of Vietnam.

Hanoi has a subtropical climate with greater percentage of humidity, which means that precipitation occurs a lot in this part of Vietnam. The region experiences two seasons – summer which is very hot and humid and winter which is relatively cold and dry. The rainy season in Hanoi occurs from May to September with an average of 200mm of rainfall is expected each month. This is a lot of rain by Western standards, so travellers who do not want to experience heavy to torrential rainfall must prevent from traveling during these months. From January to April, the climate is a little bit more chilly than normal. The average daily temperature is around 20°C or 70°F, while the average amount of rainfall is 50mm per month. It is in April when the rainy season begins so if you plan to go to Hanoi the best months are January to March.

How to Get to Hanoi from Ho Chi Minh City

Ho Chi Minh City, or better known as Saigon, became a popular tourist destination first than Hanoi. Foreigners who travel south of Vietnam usually discover that there is another picturesque destination north of Vietnam, and probably only find out at that moment that it also happens to be the capital of the country. These curious travellers more often t find their way from south to north by merely asking internet café owners or hotel receptionists. Now that Hanoi is the second most visited city in Vietnam, it should be good to know how to connect yourself from HCMC to Hanoi.

By Bus:

There is such a thing as an Open Bus here in Vietnam that can take you from Saigon to Hanoi. There are two kinds of Open Buses – the Sitting Bus and the Sleeper Bus. Let me first explain what an Open Bus is. Open Bus is a system by which your bus ticket can be used in the next bus stops in between your origin and final destination. This means that you can spend a night in one of the bus stops and just continue your journey the following day without extra charge on your end. You do have to remember that the geographical situation of Vietnam is long and narrow, which means that traveling from the south to the north may take up to days. The next thing you have to know about these Open Buses is the destinations and their stops in between. There are no direct bus companies that travel from Ho Chi Minh to Hanoi. This is the reason why the Open Bus system is feasible in this kind of situation. From Ho Chi Minh, the least number of stops that you can get is 4 until you reach Hanoi. This route takes you from Ho Chi Minh to Nha Trang, from Nha Trang to Hoi An, from Hoi An to Hue, and from Hue to Hanoi. You might then be wondering what a Sitting Bus is and what a Sleeper Bus is? Well the answer is quite literal. A Sitting Bus has seats that can only recline partially while the Sleeper Bus has seats that are fully reclined. For such a long journey like this, it is highly recommended that you take the Sleeper Bus. A ticket from Ho Chi Minh to Hanoi usually costs $50 per person which is a great deal for low budget travellers.

The next question that needs to be answered regarding the local bus system here in Vietnam is what you can expect from the travel. Don't you worry; there will be no sugar-coating involved in the answer. The answer is simple – You get what you paid for. Cheap means low quality and service. First, do not be mesmerized by the promises that you will hear from some of our local travel agents, especially if it's along the backpacker's area in Saigon. All their promises will be gone as soon as you purchase the ticket. The quality and cleanliness of the buses are a hit and miss type. You will be extra lucky if the bus has a decent, functioning restroom and if the cots or seats are sanitized. It is best to bring wet wipes or alcohol and tissue to wipe the cots before you hop on to it. Second, do not rely on the listed bus schedule because those are just very rough estimates of when the bus will arrive/leave the next bus stop. Once you start your journey, the driver usually picks up local passengers or delivers packages to destinations that are off the route. This further delays your arrival to your next destination. Third, if you are a Westerner and your body size is far from an Asian body type, expect to have an uncomfortable time in the bus. The cots and seats are designed for an Asian body type so if your legs are long, you might not fit comfortably on the sleeper bus. Lastly, take good care of your valuables.

People do fall asleep during these long journeys and some pickpockets use this to their advantage. These serve only as mere warnings. If you want to prevent these events from happening, go to the more decent and credible travel agencies in Ho Chi Minh.

By Train:

The best and most comfortable train line from Saigon to Hanoi is the Reunification Express Train. There are four Reunification Express Trains that depart to and from Saigon at different schedules to give clients different options. These four express trains are train numbers SE2, SE 4, SE6, and SE8. All these coaches depart from Saigon daily; 2 of which depart in the morning and two at night. Travel time to HCMC to Hanoi is no less than 34 hours. Since the travel time is very long, it is highly recommended that you choose the soft berth sleeping cabin for better space and comfort. Each soft berth cabin is good for four passengers, so if you are alone or with a friend, expect to share the space with a stranger.

If you are still on a tight budget but is also thinking of safety and comfort, then you should take the train rather than the bus. Aside from the shorter travel time, these new trains are relatively cleaner and better maintained that the rugged buses. The price may be a little bit more expensive but the additional cost will be worth it.

Why is the train a better option than the bus? First, because it travels faster. Second, because it is newer and better maintained, so you can expect it to be a lot cleaner than the bus. Third, because the railway passes through some of the more scenic spots in Vietnam. Lastly, trains cannot stop midway just to pick up or drop off passengers or packages. This means that trains stick to their time-tables.

By Air:

If the budget is not a hindrance, then the safest and the fastest option to get to Hanoi is by air. Instead of enduring 34 hours of train ride or more than 48 hours of bus ride, you can reach Hanoi comfortably in 2 hours. There are some budget airlines that can fly you to Hanoi with fares closely comparable to the express train fares if you book ahead of time. If not, the cheapest roundtrip ticket from Saigon to Hanoi is probably around $150 to $200, which includes checked baggage. Some of the budget and regular airlines that fly daily to and from Hanoi are Jetstar, Vietnam Airlines, VietJet Air, and Hahn Air.

Chapter 6: Where To Stay In Hanoi

Recommended Budget Hotels

Vietnam is not an expensive place so when you select budget hotels, this really means cheap yet decent places to stay in.

Little Hanoi Hostels:

A group of simple hostels in Hanoi, this company has three different branches in Hanoi – Little Hanoi Hostel 1, Little Hanoi Hostel 2, and Little Hanoi Diamond. All the three branches are within walking distance from one another however each hostel features something unique to give the guests some options. All bookings with this chain of hotels come with free breakfast and free access to the internet. There are also tour packages offered to make visits to Halong Bay or city tours much more convenient for the guests.

Little Hanoi Hostel 1 is situated within the old quarter of Hanoi. Guests who have stayed in this hostel have given rave reviews about its location and its proximity to tourists' landmarks such as the water puppets show, the Hoan Kiem Lake and the old Hanoi streets. It also provides a variety of rooms from single occupancy to family rooms and even the budget dormitory rooms.

Little Hanoi Hostel 2 is located right in front of Hoan Kiem Lake which offers an excellent view day and night. Similar to Hostel 1, this second branch is situated at the core of the old quarter of Hanoi, which makes all other tourist spots within walking distance. Aside from this, the hotel is near banks and other commercial centers. All single, double, and twin occupancy rooms offered in Hostel 2 has an old, wooden, classic feel to it.

Little Hanoi Diamond is still located at the core of Hanoi's old quarter and is within walking distance to a lot of tourist landmarks. Guests who want to have a more pampered feel may opt to stay in Little Hanoi Diamond and choose between the standard or De

Luxe rooms offered for single, double, triple, or family occupancies.

Recommended Mid-Range Hotels

Holiday Gold Hotel:

Strategically located at the center of Hanoi's old quarter, Holiday Gold Hotel offers guests 30 standard rooms and suites that are complete with amenities such as air conditioning, cable television, minibar, free access to internet, private bathroom, and many more. Its good location allows guests to conveniently walk to tourists spots such as the water puppet show, shopping areas, and the famous Hoan Kiem Lake. Holiday Gold can accommodate lone travellers, couples, and even families and can offer very reasonable and affordable rates from $28 to $55 per night. All guests are entitled to its free daily breakfast and complimentary tea or coffee.

Holiday Diamond Hotel:

Belonging to a sister company of Holiday Gold, this hotel has 19 well-designed and spacious rooms that will make its guests feel at home and comfortable. Since there are only 19 rooms in this hotel, guests can expect the service to be personalized and spot-on. Aside from its great service, Holiday Diamond Hotel is also centrally located at the old quarter of Hanoi which gives guests a more convenient way to tour the heart of this capital city. Rooms for single, double, triple, and family occupants are available for a very reasonable price range. This includes breakfast, complimentary coffee or tea, and free internet access.

Recommended Luxury Hotels

Sofitel Legend Metropole Hanoi:

Rated the best luxury hotel by travellers, Sofitel Legend Metropole offers its guests a trip down to memory lane through its tastefully refurbished and restored French colonial structure. The hotel's building dates back to 1901, when a couple of French investors decided to build this magnificent white structure laced with classy iron works. After the war, the structure was restored and was converted into a luxurious hotel and was eventually assigned by the local government as the official hotel for visiting VIPs and dignitaries.

There are a number of interesting rooms and suites offered at Sofitel Legend. At the Opera Wing, guests can choose from the premium room to the grand prestige suite all of which gives guest a clear view of the famous Opera House. At the Metropole Wing, guests can choose to stay in the luxury or the grand luxury rooms all of which are laced with classy Asian products such as silk and Mahogany furniture. Lastly at the Legendary Suites, guests can choose to check in the Graham Green Suite, Charlie Chaplin Suite, or the Somerset Maugham Suite. All of these luxurious suites will give its guests a feeling of nostalgia by its classic French colonial design partnered with modern Asian twists.

JW Marriot Hotel:

Rated as the second best luxury hotel in Hanoi by travellers, JW Marriot Hotel offers its guests a very modern feel to contrast the very classic feel of the old quarter Hanoi. The very modern architecture of JW Marriot took in consideration two things which hotel guests always look for in a hotel room – space and view. All the rooms offered by this hotel have at least 48m2 worth of space and floor to ceiling windows that offer a panoramic view of Hanoi. This hotel is highly recommended for vacationing families and even executives who are in Hanoi for business.

Chapter 7: What To Eat And Drink In Hanoi

Hanoi is a food destination. Every nook and cranny of its narrow streets are filled with food carts, hole-in-a-wall restaurants, and local cafes. You would be missing out a lot if you do not try at least one of the capital's local delicacies.

Pho (Fer)

When you are in Vietnam, you can't avoid eating pho. Pho literally translates to noodles made from rice. These noodles are cooked in beef broth mixed with select spices such as star anise, cinnamon bark, and cloves, and served with thinly sliced beef or chicken with coriander leaves, mung bean sprouts, onions, basil, and mint leaves. The pho served in Hanoi may have a slightly different taste as in Saigon or Hue or any parts of Vietnam for that matter. Each city or province in Vietnam has their very own yet similar version of pho. If you are into beef, simply say pho bo; however, if you prefer chicken, simply say pho ga.

Best Pho Restaurants in Hanoi:

• Pho Thin Restaurant

This restaurant has received rave reviews from locals as well as foreigners for their best tasting pho. Located at 13 Lo Duc street at the Hai Ba Trung District in Hanoi, Pho Thin is just a hole-in-a-wall eatery with its name written on a small signage placed beside towering stock pots. When you get past the kitchen and the stock pots, you will see small chairs facing the walls where stainless steel ledges are installed to give more eating spaces for the customers who are waiting in line to be seated. The restaurant is open from lunch time until late in the evening. Expect to wait in line but be patient enough because it is worth the wait.

● Pho Bat Dan

Its name does not translate to any fancy or profound meaning. This restaurant is named after the street where it is located — Bat Dan. Make sure to go to 49 Bat Dan street in Hanoi and you will definitely have a pho-ntastic treat! This place is famous for their pho bo or beef noodle soup with a side of veggies and lime wedges. There are 3 kinds of pho bo at this restaurant: Pho Tai Nam which means the noodle soup will be served with prime beef meat, Pho Tai which means the thinly sliced beef meat will be placed in the boiling soup stock raw as it is served to you, and the Pho Chin which means the beef is precooked before it is put on the boiling soup stock. Do not be fooled by the clarity of the soup stock because it might appear bland or tasteless but this clear soup is packed with hours and hours of hard labor and preparation. The soup stock is very clear because the restaurant's cooks have meticulously taken out the scum and impurities expelled by the beef bones used for the stock. A giant bowl of pho bo only costs $2.40 - $3.00.

Banh Mi

This famous Vietnamese food is a remnant of the strong French influence from the years of being under the French Colonial rule in the 17th century. Banh Mi is short baguette filled with Asian flavors like liver pate, fish cakes, cold cuts, pickled vegetables, hot green pepper, and other flavorings. You do not have to put all the ingredients to your Banh Mi; some locals give foreigners options on what to put in the baguette.

Best Banh Mi Restaurants:

- Banh Mi 25

Located at 25 Hang Ca street in the Hoan Kiem District, this famous Banh Mi kiosk stands by the sidewalk and surrounded by small, blue plastic chairs and tables for the customer's use. The stall is maintained by a Vietnamese couple who carefully makes the fillings which make their Banh Mi taste great. It is very filling to the stomach but not draining on the budget. To make sure that you are on the right kiosk, look for the

Trip Advisor seal that is posted on the glass stand and on the big menu.

● Xuc Xich Ran

This is actually not the name of the Banh Mi stall, instead this is the kind of Banh Mi that is served here. This Banh Mi stand serves a soft yet crunchy baguette filled with fillets of fried chicken meat with picked carrots, radish, and many more. This tiny stall is located along Ma May street near the backpacker's area in Hanoi. The stall stands in front of an open hair salon. Be patient enough to look for this Banh Mi stand because it has a unique filling which you cannot find elsewhere.

Bun Cha

Bun Cha is a lunch and dinner staple in every Vietnamese household. Bun Cha literally translates to vermicelli noodles and fatty pork. It is a combination of grilled pork wrapped in lettuce with slices of unripe papaya fruit, thin vermicelli rice noodles, and other fresh Vietnamese herbs. The appetizing smell of this sizzling grub along the streets of Hanoi will surely make you crave for it.

Best Bun Cha Restaurants:

● Bun Cha Nem Cua Be Dac Kim Restaurant

Located at 67 Duong Thang Street in the heart of the Old Quarter of Hanoi, this restaurant serves one of the best Bun Cha dishes in this capital city. In this restaurant you may order your Bun Cha fix dry or wet. When it's dry, your Bun Cha will be served on a plate with a hill of vermicelli noodles or rice, with a hearty amount of green veggies on the side, and a bowl of Vietnam's famous dipping sauce. When it is wet, your Bun Cha will be served in a bowl with a generous amount of vermicelli noodles soaked in tasty soup stock similar to pho. However you want to eat your Bun Cha, you will surely be satisfied by the tender, smoky flavour of the pork.

Vietnamese Egg Coffee

Everywhere you go around Vietnam, you will see tiny stalls that sell the famous Ca Phe Sua Da or iced coffee with condensed milk. This is a staple drink for the locals. They drink coffee at any time of the day. In Hanoi, the more famous coffee drink is topped with egg yolk. Yes, it is a delicacy here in Hanoi and a lot of foreigners have taken a liking to it too.

Best Egg Coffee Shops:

- Giang Café

Located in a very hard-to-find area in Hanoi, Giang Café has started to gain popularity amongst foreigners who travel to Hanoi. This coffee shop is constantly filled with locals who want to have a quick rest and snack on this local drink but recently Giang Café is also filled with curious travellers who want to give the drink a try.

Specifically situated at 39 Nguyen Huu Huan Street, you would have to walk down a narrow alley before you can find a sign that states where the café is. Once you are near the place, you can distinctly smell roasted coffee so you'll know you are there. Go up the stairs and seat yourself on one of the low seats available. The low seats are something familiar to Vietnamese but are something that causes difficulty for tall Caucasians; however, since there is no other choice, you would have to endure it.

Coffee here can be served warm or cold, but the warm egg coffee is better. It is frothy and thick, something that will really jolt your senses.

Chapter 8: Where To Go / What To Do In Hanoi

It is a lot easier to follow a suggested itinerary when touring an unfamiliar place so that time will not be wasted and the travel will be worth it. A minimum of 2 full days is actually needed to have a quick go around the old quarter of Hanoi and the other must-see places outside it. Here is a sample itinerary with the description of every tourist destination in Hanoi:

Day 1: Exploring the Old Quarter

Traveling to Hanoi is all about immersing yourself to the history of this simple city and understanding the past for which the present is directly attributed to. For this reason, your first day in Hanoi should be all about exploring the famous Old Quarter. Psych yourself to a lot of walking, dodging pesky motorbikes, shopping for local souvenirs and tasting the unique flavors known to Vietnam. As your itinerary revolves around the Old

Quarter, it is highly suggested that you select a hotel situated within or near the district.

There is really no set formula of where to start your journey and where to end it. Walking around the Old Quarter is more of listening to your senses and playing everything by ear. Sometimes, when there is something delectably fragrant in one narrow alleyway or a colourful item on the next, you should take the chance and go there because it might be something interesting and new which you can share to future travellers as well. Although there is no set path to take, here are the must-see landmarks within the Old Quarter that you must visit:

• Ho Chi Minh Mausoleum

This is a memorial land devoted to one of the iconic figures in the history of Vietnam, Ho Chi Minh. This heroic icon was the leader of the Communist Party of Vietnam who fought for the country's unification and freedom. Albeit the gruesome and bloody period known as the Vietnam War, Ho Chi Minh was able to regain freedom for the Vietnamese citizens. When the beloved hero died, a memorial hall was built for him where his remains rest and can be viewed by people from all over the world. This memorial hall is right at the center of Ba Dinh Square. If looking at a well-preserved body in a glass case is something that is not too morbid for you, then head right in the mausoleum. This mausoleum is usually open to the public from 9:00am to 12:00nn only. Another must see activity here is the changing of the guards.

You must take note that there is a strict dress code that must be followed to be allowed inside the hall. Visitors must wear long pants or skirts. Also, while inside the building, both hands must be placed in the pockets of the pants or arms should be crossed across the chest to ensure that nothing is touched or taken. Cameras, food, and drinks are also not allowed within the mausoleum.

● Ho Chi Minh Museum

Located just right next to the mausoleum is the Ho Chi Minh Museum. This structure was built in the 1990s to commemorate the life and the works of Ho Chi Minh. This is a nice place to visit especially if you want to know more about the history of Vietnam during the mid-20th century.

● Imperial Citadel of Thang Long

Declared as World Heritage Site by UNESCO in 2010, the Royal Citadel provides a window to the past which the locals take pride of. This structure also provides proof of how advanced was the Vietnamese civilization during the 9th to the 18th centuries. At this very site, some excavations were made where a lot of archaeological artifacts were discovered.

Most of the original structures of the Imperial Citadel have been destroyed during the French Colonial regime, but the Cua Bac or the North Gate of the once enormous palace still remain standing. This structure is now open to the public every day, except Mondays. Going here is a little bit out of place, so you can hire a taxi or rickshaw to bring you to Citadel.

Street Shopping

● Hang Gai Street or Silk Street

Another must-see place in the Old Quarter is the Hang Gai Street. This short street connects Hang Dao and Hang Bong. This is a street lined with small shops that sell anything and everything local and unique to Vietnam. If you want to get the best silk products or clothing, this is the place to go to. You can easily find products made from silk like table cloths, placemats, dresses, and many more. You do have to expect that the prices of the products sold along Hang Gai are quite expensive because this is a tourist spot.

● Ba Trieu Street

Located in the Old Quarter, this street has the best and finest ceramics shops. For limitless choices, look for Quang's Ceramics Store. This shop's ceramics are designed elegantly and priced reasonably.

• Nha Tho Street

Vietnam is popular for its lacquerware – this is a natural resin derived from the Lacquer Tree that naturally varnishes wood, stone, or porcelain. Some of the lacquerware sold in Vietnam are handmade by the locals who have disabilities as a means of livelihood. For a variety of lacquerware decors and furniture, find Delta Deco store along Nha Tho Street.

• Hang Dau Street

This street is also known as the Shoe Heaven in Hanoi. Located closer to the lake, this street has a variety of men's and ladies' shoes to offer. Some are locally made while others are Chinese bootlegs, but all of the items are sold here at a good bargain. However if your shoe size is 10 US and above, do not expect to find an available pair for you. Shopping here in Hanoi still has not adjusted to the Caucasian sizes. There are other stores along this street that sell clothing so devote ample time walk through this area.

Hoan Kiem Lake

At the heart of the historic site of Hanoi, the Hoan Kiem Lake is a prime scenic spot in Hanoi. When you are at Hanoi, you must visit this paradise. Hoan Kiem Lake means Lake of the Returned Sword. This name was derived from a famous legend about Le Loi, who was boating on the lake met a Golden Turtle God that asked for his Golden Sword. Until today, there are soft-shelled turtles that can be spotted around the lake.

At the northern part of the lake, you can find the Temple of the Jade which was built in the 1700s. This temple is built on a small island called Jade Island which you can access by crossing a red bridge. At the center of the lake, another structure, the Turtle Tower, was built to commemorate the legend of Le Loi and the Golden Turtle God. You must see this lake especially at night to see the wonderful light display around it.

Day 2: Outside Hanoi

If the heart of Hanoi is a cultural, heritage site, its outskirt is a natural gem. Travellers in Hanoi can easily access one of the seven natural wonders of the world, Ha Long Bay. Declared by UNESCO as a natural heritage site, Ha Long Bay is 170km east or 3 ½ hours from Hanoi. The word Ha Long came from a legendary tale about dragons descending from the sea; therefore it literally means dragons descending from the sea. This is a must-see destination; one must not leave Hanoi not going to Ha Long Bay.

How to Get to Ha Long Bay

The easiest way to get to Ha Long Bay is by booking with a credible travel agent in advance. Being part of the 7 Natural Wonders of the World has increased the amount of tourists to Ha Long, so this needs advance booking. When you book with a travel agent, your transfers to and from Ha Long Bay as well as your Ha Long Bay Cruise should be pre-arranged by them.

Find a Reputable Travel Agent:

The quality of tour that you will receive and that you must expect is dependent on the amount that you are willing to spend on the cruise. Some travel agencies offer an afternoon of cruise while others offer an overnight package. You really don't need to spend a night in Ha Long because an afternoon of sightseeing should be enough to cover the good parts.

You should also understand that it is not really bad to book with budget travel agencies. What makes their prices cheap is that when they book clients, they find cheap cruise companies that can still accommodate passengers. You will still get to experience the beauty of Ha Long Bay; however you do not have any choice regarding the itinerary and the food. Budget travel agencies usually charge $40 per person which includes transfers. If you want your tour to be a little bit more personalized, then look for a travel agency that offers a mid-range price of around $80 per head. You must also check the travel agency's credibility by searching for reviews online or even by interviewing other tourists you meet in Hanoi. Word-of-mouth advertisements should be your best ally. If you really want a top-of-the-line tour and want to spend a night on Ha Long Bay, then you can go for the A-list tour operators that charge around $400 per person per night.

Do-It-Yourself Tour of Ha Long Bay:

If you really want to have a hands-on feel for your Ha Long Bay tour, you can choose to create your own itinerary. You can reach Ha Long Bay by taking a bus to Ha Long City or more known as Bai Chai. From there you can hire a cab that can take you to the harbour. At the harbour, you can book a Ha Long Bay Cruise with any of the operators on site. The only downside to this plan is that you may find a cheap cruise but might have to pay more for the food and drinks on board. What might be your better alternative is to hire a boat that can take you to Cat Ba Island. When you get to the island, you can decide how long you want to stay and explore around. Remember, though, that if you do not have plans of staying over at Ha Long, you need to get back to Bai Chai early so that you can catch a bus back to Hanoi. When you actually think about it, booking with a travel agent is really the best option.

Things to Consider:

Weather is one of the things to consider when planning a trip to Ha Long Bay. The best time to visit Ha Long Bay is when the weather is warm and dry and that is during October to April. If you are planning to go sometime in January or February, it is best to check the Chinese calendar first and not plan your tour on the week of Chinese New Year or Tet for the Vietnamese. During Tet festival, everything is closed and no operator will bring you to Ha Long.

Another thing to consider are the items that you need to bring. Since this is an outdoor activity, you need to bring a strong sunblock, so that your skin will be protected. You also need to bring an anti-mosquito patch or lotion just to make sure you don't get bitten by an insect. Lastly, you need to bring water. Water is served during the cruise but it is best to bring your own bottle.

Chapter 9: Saigon Or Ho Chi Minh City

Ho Chi Minh City (HCMC) is the largest and densest city in Vietnam. Many foreigners actually mistake HCMC as the capital city because of its popularity and bustling ambience. This city is named after the famous Vietnamese leader Ho Chi Minh after merging the South of Vietnam to the central region. Prior to this name, this city was known as Saigon. This name is still widely used by locals and foreigners because this name was even made popular by the famous Broadway musical, Miss Saigon.

History

Saigon is surrounded by two major bodies of water, Saigon River and the Mekong River. Since rivers are essential in creative a civilized community, Saigon was inhabited by fisher folks coming from the Khmer region or what we know now as Cambodia. When the Vietnamese settlers came in the late 1700s, they pushed the Khmer people away from the center of Saigon to the banks of the Mekong river. When Vietnam was conquered by France, Saigon was declared as the capital of the colony called Cochinchina. After the Second World War, Saigon became the capital of the South of Vietnam, which eventually merged with the greater Vietnam.

Climate

It is generally hot in HCMC. Tour guides in Saigon actually love to joke that there are only two seasons in this region, warm and warmer. It is actually true. The average daily temperature in a given year is between 27°C to 31°C, with an average humidity of 80% while the average amount of rainfall per month is around 150mm. The daily temperature, as well as the amount of rainfall spikes during the months of May to October when the rainy season occurs. The best time to travel to Saigon is between the months of November to April, when the weather is slightly cooler and the expected amount of rainfall is lesser.

Chapter 10: Where To Stay In Saigon

Recommended Budget Hotels

There are many budget hotels and run-off-the-house type of hostels at the backpackers' area in Saigon. This area is found in District 1, more specifically along the Pham Ngu Lao street and its adjacent streets. This area is conveniently located near famous landmarks, like the Ben Thanh Market and the Fine Arts Museum. Since this is a backpackers' area, it is lined with a lot of noisy clubs and bars that may not be a good location for families or travellers who want to have a relaxing evening.

● Galaxy Hotel & Capsule

Located along De Tham Street is Galaxy Hotel & Capsule. This unique hotel does not only offer the usual single, double, and family rooms but also offers the Japanese inspired capsule beds. Unlike the Japanese version, this hotel's capsule looks more like bunk beds put in one dorm room. Male and female occupants may take the capsule; however, they have shared bathrooms and toilets. Guests have access to a safe to keep their valuables, like wallets and passports. It is a very cheap option. If you still prefer the regular rooms, Galaxy Hotel's has clean rooms for a single passenger and family groups, which are a little more expensive.

● Diep Anh Guesthouse

Situated along Pham Ngu Lao Street, Diep Anh is not your ordinary kind of hostel. This is a house run by a sweet Vietnamese couple Diep and Anh. They have opened their doors to foreigners who want to have a home away from their homes. At Diep Anh you may not get the usual facilities offered in a hotel but who cares? This place is squeaky clean, the rooms are spacious and the service is top-notch. Plus, and to top it off, Diep and Anh can be your personal tour guides. They are always ready to answer every query and will make sure you get to where you want to go using the correct public transportation system in Saigon. This place has a cheap price for a great service.

Recommended Mid-Range Hotels

If you want to have a quieter ambience, then you better stay away from the backpackers' area and move closer to the center of District 1. There are many mid-range hotels away from Pham Ngu Lao and even closer to famous landmarks like the Reunification Palace and the Ho Chi Minh Museum.

● Lavender Hotel

There are two Lavender Hotels in the first District of HCMC. The main branch, Lavender Central, is located along the main street Le Than Thon which is just a stone's throw away from Ben Thanh Market and walking distance from the Reunification Palace and War Remnants Museum.

The second branch, Lavender Boutique, is located along Ly Tu Trong Street which is also walking distance from Ben Thanh Market.

Hotel Majestic

Located in the upper class area of Saigon along Dong Khoi Street, Hotel Majestic offers its guests a great view of the famous Saigon River. Aside from the great view, the hotel itself is part of the city's history as it was built and established in the 1920s. Each room in this hotel is a window to the past with dark teak wood furniture, yet still reflects the present.

Recommended Luxury Hotels

Hotel Nikko

Situated at the heart of Saigon's business center, Hotel Nikko is voted the best luxury hotel in Saigon. There is no doubt to this review because this hotel is complete with amenities such as international restaurants, spa, fitness center, and a swimming pool that shows a panoramic view of Saigon. This hotel is best suited for executives who are in Saigon for business, yet would still want to be close to the city's famous landmarks. This hotel is just a 10-minute drive to Reunification Palace, Ho Chi Minh Museum, and the War Remnants Museum. It is also a few minutes from Ben Thanh Market.

● Intercontinental Asiana

If you want a luxury hotel treatment but not spend as much, then you must stay at Intercontinental Asiana. Located at the upper class area of Saigon, this hotel is close to famous landmarks such as the Opera House, Post Office of Saigon and the Notre Dame Cathedral. It is also closely situated to the nicer shopping centers like Parkson and Vincom Center.

Chapter 11: Getting Around In Saigon

Walk

The best way to get around the tourist area of Saigon is by walking. Aside from saving costs, walking helps you see every activity, every hidden landmark and every sumptuous food cart along the busy streets of Saigon. It is generally safe to walk here in the morning and at night so you can really venture out and enjoy the sceneries. The only unsafe activity that pedestrians have to live by every single day is crossing the street. Thousands of motorbikes cruise along the major and minor streets of Saigon which makes crossing difficult for tourists. You will really need a lot of courage and confidence when crossing. Don't worry; these bikers will not hit you so follow Johnny Walker's mantra: Keep Walking.

Motorbike/Bicycle

A cheap way to traverse the streets of Saigon is by renting a scooter or a bicycle. Although cheap, the risk is great. If you are not that keen on driving a 2-wheeled vehicle, then better not rent one. However, if you are an experienced biker and have a heart of steel then you might even enjoy renting one.

There are many pros as well as cons in renting a bike in Saigon. The advantages are you can cut down transportation costs and cut down travel time; therefore you can see more landmarks or shops. The disadvantages are risking your life and limited parking space. Please do weigh the pros and cons before you decide on renting a bike.

Taxi

Tourists who have read about Saigon prior to venturing out here must have read a lot of words of caution about taking a taxi in Saigon. Again, do not worry. Generally it is safe but not all taxi companies are as credible and honest as others. Some taxi drivers will insist on setting a fixed amount especially with tourists, while other companies have meters that run as fast as a horse.

Please do take note of the following credible taxi companies:

Vinasun – white Toyota Innova

Mai Linh - white and green cars or minivans

Vinataxi – yellow cars

Saigon Tourist – white and pink cars

PetroVietnam – seldom seen in Saigon but guaranteed honest drivers and meters

Chapter 10: Where To Eat In Saigon

As mentioned in the chapter that featured Hanoi, Vietnam is a food destination. All of the must-eat cuisines mentioned in that chapter are available in Saigon as well. You can easily find banh mi, pho, bun cha, and Vietnamese coffee. Here are some of the best restaurants that you must try:

● Quan Anh Ngon 138

Located at 138 Nam Ky Khoi Nghia St., this restaurant is housed inside a yellow mansion-like building which can accommodate hundreds of guests. Despite its big area it is always filled with happy patrons. What is special about this restaurant is its crew. The owner of Quan Anh Ngon has employed experienced street vendors to ensure quality of food and service. Some of the stations of its cooks are even outside the kitchen to show the customers how some of the meals are prepared. You must try their barbeque pork, fresh spring rolls, pho and their Vietnamese crepe called banh xeo.

● Lemongrass

If you want to experience a classy version of local cuisines then head to Lemongrass. Situated at 4 Nguyen Thiep Street near the Dong Khoi area, Lemongrass is a small, quaint restaurant that can serve up to 50 customers. Service and food here are excellent and complemented by the French-inspired displays and mood lighting. This is best for dating couples or small family reunions. Before heading out to Lemongrass, it is best to make reservations as it might be full, especially at night. You can ask you hotel's receptionist to do that for you.

You must try the restaurant's version of fresh and fried spring rolls, steamed crabs, fried shrimp, and their scallop rice. You will surely have a happy stomach after a meal in Lemongrass.

● Quan 94

If you are craving for crabs but do not have a hefty budget, this problem will be solved going to Quan 94. This no-frills restaurant only has stainless tables partnered with old plastic stools. Operated by three old women, Quan 94 is the cheapest way to satisfy your crustacean cravings. Do not be fooled though; there are many copy cats but these copy cats have colourful lighting or have hard selling waiters. If you see those Quan 94's, you need to know they are faux. The real deal has a very unassuming ambience but great food. The bestseller here is their soft-shelled crab. Quan 94 is located at 94 Dien Tien Hoang, District 1.

● Lunch Lady

Even Anthony Bourdain forgot his name when he tried the pork knuckles soup of the famous Lunch Lady, Nguyen Thi Thanh. Her business is not even in a market or a restaurant. Her eatery is established on a sidewalk which sheltered by a tree but once you taste the soup, you will forget where you are or even the domestic dogs that are staring at you. Do not expect anyone chatting with you in English. She is quite aloof because of the language barrier but once you take a seat in one of her small plastic stools, she will immediately serve you with fresh spring rolls and a bowl of pho-ntastic pork soup. As for the price, she will write everything down on piece of paper but it's not really that expensive.

● Pho 2000

This is a famous chain of restaurants in Ho Chi Minh City but the most popular branch is the one beside Ben Thanh Market. Pho is obviously its bestseller but their fried spring rolls and chicken curry with baguette are to die for too. You would also love to go back to this restaurant because the prices are so cheap yet the servings are generous.

● Trung Nguyen and Highlands Coffee

Coffee is a staple drink for the Vietnamese. Trung Nguyen and Highlands Coffee are the two more popular brands that serve the best Vietnamese coffee with condensed milk. Even when the world was craving for Starbucks, Saigon locals and tourists continuously flock these coffee shops.

Chapter 12: What To Do/Where To Go In Saigon

What is nice about Saigon, which is similar to Hanoi, is that everything is within walking distance. If you love to just walk around and enjoy the sights and ambience of a new place, then Saigon is the best destination for you. Where ever you stay, for as long as you are within the 1st District, you will be able to easily see all the famous landmarks of Saigon. There are also a couple of must-see destinations that are an hour or two away from Saigon. All these will be discussed in an itinerary or schedule form so that your time in Saigon will be well spent.

Three days in Saigon should be enough to have a look around the city and to be able to explore its outskirts. Here is a suggested itinerary for you:

Day 1: Saigon City Tour

As soon as you get to your hotel, get settled and prepare to walk around the city.

Reunification Palace:

Previously known as the Independence Palace, the Reunification Palace was the official home and office of the head of the Southern Vietnam during the 1940s when Vietnam was still divided into 2 separate states. Now that Vietnam is unified, this structure is no longer a symbol of division instead a symbol of unity and cooperation.

The Reunification Palace is open to the public from Monday to Friday, 7:30am to 5:00pm with an hour and a half of lunch break in between. A very modest entrance fee is required to all visitors. You will probably need an hour to go around the hall by yourself but a little bit longer if you will join the tour guide.

The palace is located at 135 Nam Ky Khoi Nghia Street which is walking distance from Dong Khoi.

War Remnants Museum:

A few paces away from the Reunification Palace is the War Remnants Museum. If the Reunification Palace is a reminder of positivity amongst the locals, the War Remnants Museum is entirely the opposite. This museum showcases the horrid effect of the Vietnam War which emphasizes on the negative effect brought about by the meddling of the Americans. If you are traveling with children, this place should not be part of your itinerary. However, if you are all mature adults and are really curious about Vietnam's recent past, then go and visit War Remnants. Expect to find vivid pictures of the victims of the war; some are even coloured, which can be a little too morbid. If you are an American who wishes to visit, get ready to read negative descriptions about the Americans who fought in the war.

If you are coming from the Reunification Palace and want to proceed to this museum, walk west towards Vo Van Tan Street. Turn left at Vo Van Tan and you will see the museum right away. The museum is open from 7:30am to 5:00pm, with an hour and a half of lunch break. There is also a modest admission fee.

Museum of Ho Chi Minh City:

If the War Remnants Museum is too intimidating for you, you can proceed right away to the Museum of Ho Chi Minh City. Do not confuse this museum with the Ho Chi Minh Museum located closer to the backpacker's area. The Museum of Ho Chi Minh City houses artifacts and memorabilia from the Vietnam war. Some of the exhibits show a collection of armaments and weapons, which show the hardships the nation had to go through to overcome the war. What is nice about this museum is that it is house inside what was then a Governor's Palace. The structure was built in the late 1800s following the design of French architect, Alfred Foulhoux.

To reach this museum coming from the Reunification Palace, walk east along Nam Ky Khoi Nghia towards Ly Tu Trong Street. Once you reach Ly Tu Trong, turn left and you will see the museum on your right. The museum is open from Monday to Sunday, 8:00am to 5:00pm with a minimal admission fee.

Ben Thanh Market:

Cho Ben Thanh or Ben Thanh Market is an iconic figure in Saigon where most locals and tourists converge to buy essential items such as food, clothing and much more. All the food items sold in the market are properly zoned – the fresh ingredients are found in one corner, the dry ingredients are found in the opposite corner, the sundries are in the opposite end. You can find almost anything and everything in Ben Thanh. From souvenir shirts that cost less than $5.00 each, knock off signature bags, variety of shoes and sandals, to selection upon selection of coffee beans, all these are found in the market. You can also find a lot of quick bites which you can snack on the spot. Try their version of pho, bun cha, and banh mi. The day market opens at 6am and closes at 6pm.

If you thought the market is boring at night, you thought wrong. Once the sun has set, the market transforms into a street market bustling with a lot of good local cuisine. You can just sit at any table and order from any of the food concessionaires nearby. You will be amazed at how keen on remembering your order and your table the waiters are. You must try the local snails cooked in coconut cream; they are to die for!

Sinh Café:

This is a café cum budget travel agency that offers tourists cheaper alternatives to the must-see sights in and around Saigon. Sinh Café is located at De Tham, Pham Ngu Lao right at the heart of the backpackers' area. You may choose to go here before or after the market, but it is important that you go here before the night falls so that you can secure a booking for your journey the following day.

Once you get to Sinh Café, inquire about the full day tour to Cu Chi Tunnel and Cao Dai Temple. You might be wondering what these are. These two important historic sites are included in the second day in Saigon.

Sinh Café offers very affordable rates to Cu Chi and Cao Dai. Inclusive to the fee are your transfers to and from the tour sites, tour guide, and a bottle of water. What is exclusive is the entrance fee to Cu Chi Tunnel.. Once you book the tour, the agent will tell you what time you need to be at Sinh Café the following day to meet up with your other tour mates.

Day 2: Cu Chi Tunnels and Cao Dai Temple Full Day Tour

When you are in Saigon, you must not miss the Cu Chi Tunnel and Cao Dai Temple tour. It is very easy to book a tour out of the center of Saigon because at just about every corner in District 1 is a credible travel agency. But as suggested above, it is best to head to Pham Ngu Lao and book a cheap tour in any of the budget travel agencies there. Sinh café is one of the more famous and reliable travel agencies in the area. If you have successfully booked a tour with this agency, then for sure they will require you to be outside the café by 8am to meet up with the other tourists who booked the same tour. Before you depart, you will be greeted by your tour guide and led to the bus that will bring you outside Saigon. Vietnamese naturally have a hard time speaking in English because there are just some letters that are difficult to pronounce, so please be patient and listen carefully to the assigned guide.

Cu Chi Tunnels:

The district of Cu Chi, located about an hour and a half away from the 1st district of Saigon, was heavily affected during the Vietnam War. This site was used as a hideout for thousands of Vietnamese soldiers and civilians that fought and escaped the wrath of the war. You might wonder how a land with lush greeneries can hide thousands of locals. Well, due to the innovativeness and probably the survival instincts of the Vietnamese, these men and women were able to dig out kilometres and kilometres of tunnels similar to a network of subway lines except these tunnels were very narrow, damp and humid. It was actually thanks to these tunnels that the Vietnamese were able to weaken the power of the Americans and eventually were able to banish them from Cu Chi. Up to this day the Vietnamese government was able to preserve more than 120 kilometers of these tunnels, one of which is open to the more adventurous tourists.

The Cu Chi Tunnels Camp is open from Monday to Saturday, 9:00am to 5:00pm and the entrance fee is very cheap. Your tour guide will lead you to the entrance, which is a wide tunnel that descends towards lush scenery. Once you get into the camp, your first stop will be a video presentation of the history of Cu Chi and the Vietnam War. Also found in this audio-visual bunker is a 3-dimensional map of the tunnels in Cu Chi. After the video presentation, your guide will lead you to one of the original tunnel entrances/exits made inconspicuous by the natural foliage and dried leaves. After which you will see life-size dioramas of how life was during the war. Before proceeding to the next part of the tour, your guide will lead you inside one of the many foxholes that are actually widened and cemented to accommodate tall tourists. Despite the adjustment made on the tunnels, they still seem very small and very dark. Make sure you have a small flashlight and that you are not claustrophobic before heading down the tunnel. The last part of the tour is an outdoor shooting range where you can buy 10 AK47 or M16 bullets and try shooting these monstrous guns. You don't have to worry about recoils because the rifles are pegged onto a solid wall; however, despite being installed on a wall, you can still feel the kick every time you pull the trigger. If you are not up to shooting 10 bullets, you may ask your fellow tourists to share bullets with you. As you proceed out of the camp, you will be given free tapioca tea to drink and you can also watch how rice paper is made.

Cao Dai Temple:

About an hour away from Cu Chi is the famous Cao Dai Temple, located in the province of Tay Ninh, which is almost 100km away from the center of Saigon. Cao Dai is a native religion that mixes other major religions such as Islam, Buddhism, Christianity, Taoism and Confucianism. Aside from marrying all these religions to form one religion, Cao Dai also hail famous personalities such as Victor Hugo, Joan of Arc and Shakespeare. What is even more enthralling is the very colourful temple that represents all these beliefs. The temple was built in the 1930's and this is the biggest, most beautiful Cao Dai temple in the whole of Vietnam. A visit to this temple is usually partnered with the Cu Chi Tunnel tour because this temple is quite far from Saigon. Plus, there is really not much to do here except take pictures of idols and images inside the temple. You'll be very lucky if your visit will be at the same time as the religious ceremony of the Cao Dai followers because you can witness how they revere the "Holy See", a spherical icon with an image of an eye.

Lacquerware Store:

Some travel agencies bring tourists to a big Lacquerware store before bring them back to Saigon. As expected, the store sells very expensive items as this is considered as a tourist trap; however, it is good to know that the products sold in the warehouse are created by PWDs and this helps sustain their livelihood. There are a lot of beautiful ornaments sold here; you can buy very nice jewelry boxes, colorful home wares, and many more.

Back to Saigon City

Depending on the traffic situation, you will probably be back in the city before 6pm. You can spend the evening eating at Ben Thanh's street market or you can take a cab to Notre Dame Cathedral and spend an evening watching the locals have a night picnic outside the church or you can get a massage in any massage parlors in District 1.

Day 3: Shopping

Saigon is still not comparable with Bangkok or Hong Kong as regards to shopping, but there are some decent places where tourists can go and get good quality bags and clothes.

Saigon Square:

This haven of cheap knock-off and even original surplus bags is located along Nam Ky Khoi Nghia Street, which is actually walking distance east from the Reunification Palace. There are many reasons why tourists find Saigon Square better than Ben Thanh market - the first reason is that it is air-conditioned and well-lit. After walking under the heat of the sun, Saigon Square will be a welcome shelter to all sweaty and sun-soaked tourists. This shopping complex is not only filled with good quality, cheap bags, it is also filled with a lot of camping and mountaineering outfits. Vietnam is a country filled with western brand sweat shops like Samsonite, Quiksilver, Northface, Deuter, Crumpler, and many more, so some items that you will find in Saigon Square are actually original brands. Even the vendors are honest enough to tell you if the bag is made in Vietnam or a knock off from China.

The second reason why tourists love to shop here is most vendors accept US dollars. Not only will they accept US dollars, they also give change in dollars!

Here in Saigon Square, you don't need to work your mental math abilities to converse thousands of Dong to dollars; the vendors convert it for you.

Saigon Square is open from 8:00am to 10:00pm. You can go here early in the morning so that there will be less shoppers and the vendors are still a lot kinder, or late in the evening when the weather is a lot cooler.

Russian Market:

This shopping haven is a new addition to the growing shopping community in Saigon. Established in 1991 as part of the Saigon Tax Trade Center, the Russian Market moved into its new home at 225 Vo Van Kiet St, Ben Chuong Duong Building, District 1 in 2013. This is not exclusive to Russian products, nor Russian stores; the reason why it is called like this is because when it was still in the tax trade center most of the clients were Russian businessmen buying items in bulk and selling them in Russia.

This shopping mall also has similar items to the ones sold in Saigon Square, but the Russian Market may be a little cheaper than its famous competitor. This is truly a place full of bargains.

You can easily access this market by hailing a cab. Ask the cab driver to bring you behind the backpacker's area, by the river banks.

Cholon:

Cholon is more known as the Chinatown in Saigon. Cholon literally translates to Big Market. The most famous market in Cholon is the Binh Tay Market. Do not compare this market to the Russian Market and Saigon Square because Binh Tay is the real deal. It is an outdoor market that is full of fresh meat, fish, chicken, veggies, spices that are familiar to the Chinese palate. It is nice to wander around and try some of the authentic Chinese dim sum sold along the street. Aside from a food feast, you can also explore some of the nearby Buddhist temples that are open to the public.

Binh Tay is outside the tourist center of Saigon. You can really just access this by hailing a cab. Ask the cab driver to bring you to Cho Binh Tay in Thap Muio St, District 2. However, if you feel more adventurous, go to Benh Thanh Market and look for the nearest bus station that services Bus number 1. Bus 1 has a stop very near Binh Tay.

Traveling to Phnom Penh, Cambodia from Saigon City

A lot of tourists go to Ho Chi Minh City as a jump off point to its neighboring city Phnom Penh in Cambodia. Aside from the travel being budget friendly, Cambodia is also very near Saigon. Travel time does not take more than 3 hours and not more than 5 hours to get to Phnom Penh. It is easy to arrange a side trip to Cambodia with one of the budget tours located in the backpacker's area in Saigon. Here is how you can go to Cambodia from Saigon:

Go to any of the budget travel agencies located along Pham Ngu Lao. You can head straight to Sinh Café because they usually have the earliest departure at 6:30am to Cambodia. Have this arranged a day or two before your intended visit to Cambodia to ensure your seats. If you are not Asian, you would need to pay for your Cambodian Visas (if you don't have one yet). It is highly recommended that you discuss this first with your travel agent before confirming your tickets so that everything is laid out.

After traveling for 2 hours, you will reach the Vietnam-Cambodia border where all your personal effects will be scanned and your passports and visas checked. After this quick check and restroom stop, your journey to Phnom Penh will resume. What has improved this journey from what it used to be is the addition of a bridge at Neak Leoung. Before, buses would stop and wait for a roll-on, roll-off ferry that would bring the bus and the passengers across the Mekong River. This bridge made a lot of tourists and even tour operators very happy.

Chapter 13: Hue

Located north of Da Nang, Hue is a historical region of Vietnam. This was once the capital of the Vietnam under the imperial ruling of the Nguyen Dynasty in the 1800's to the 1900's. Since it was once a capital of what was then the turning point of Vietnam, Hue is host to a lot of cultural and historical landmarks which tourists love seeing.

How to get to Hue

From Hanoi:

If you are in Hanoi and want to have a side trip to this ancient capital, you actually have two transportation options: one can get you there for a minimal price but for 15 gruelling hours; while the other will get you there in an hour but for a greater price.

The first option is via an overnight train called the Reunification Express. Traveling by train is considered a commodity amongst the locals, as this is the only close-to-efficient system of transportation in Vietnam. If you wish to travel to Hue via train, you better buy your tickets a few days ahead to secure them; otherwise, you'll be left with the more expensive first-class seats. The cheapest train tickets to Hue will only give you a hard, economy seat. Remember that travel time to Hue is 15 hours, so I highly suggest you get a sleeper seat in 4-person cabin.

The second option is by air, which can quickly and conveniently take you to Hue in an hour. Vietnam airlines are probably the most reliable company that flies to Hue. If you want a really low rate, you need to purchase tickets months ahead.

Where to Stay

It is best to spend at least one night at Hue so that you can soak yourself in the culture and history of this ancient imperial site. Here are some of the highly recommended hostels or hotels around the area.

Jade Hotel

This budget hotel is centrally located. It is near the historic landmarks and is very lively at night due to the street markets adjacent to it. The staff and management of this hotel can speak good English and they are very hospitable and accommodating. Aside from this, Jade Hotel serves a sumptuous breakfast with a variety of fruits in season, which comes free with your booking.

Moonlight Hotel

This midrange hotel offers more amenities such as a pool, spa, fitness center and a kids club. Just established 2 years ago, Moonlight Hotel assures guests of a luxury service that is light on the budget. It is also centrally located; therefore, guests can just walk to Hue's famous landmarks.

Indochine Palace – Best Western Premier

Receive an impeccable and spotless service from the staff of Best Western Premier in Hue. With over 150 luxury rooms, this hotel has a variety of rooms from the deluxe room, studio king, 1 and 2 bedroom suites, and the grand suite. This luxurious hotel sits right at the heart of the historic part of Hue, close to the scenic Perfume River and the Royal Citadel. A night in a deluxe room includes free buffet breakfast and use of the hotel's facilities.

What to See

Travellers who visit Hue usually just spend one full day before moving on to other scenic places in Vietnam. In order to see all you need to see in this heritage site, it would be better to book a cheap, group tour in one of the budget travel agencies found in the center of Hue. One of the many travel agencies you can book a group tour with is Hue Tourist, located along Le Loi Street, or you can arrange a more private tour with Shop ∂ Go Hue.

When booking a tour, make sure it includes these following places:

• Royal Tombs

Almost everything in Hue is accessible by foot, except for the Royal Tombs. You can reach the Royal Tombs by hiring a motorbike, renting a bike or booking a group tour. There is more than one site and to see all of them, you need to make at least 3 different stops.

• Minh Mang Tomb

Built in the 1800's, the Minh Mang Tomb was made for the second emperor of the Nguyen Dynasty. When Emperor Minh Mang ordered to have his tomb built, he was already very sick. Because of his illness, his death preceded the completion of his tomb. The construction of the Tomb of Minh Mang was carried on by the successor and son, Thuie Tri. The entire compound is 18 hectares big and it houses 40 different structures consisting of pavilions, temples, palaces, and many more. Tourists who have been to this compound were always left speechless at the beauty and grandeur of the place. When visiting this complex, get ready to climb up and down the stairs and do a lot of walking.

Make sure you wear proper shoes and bring water for hydration.

● Khai Dinh Tomb

This tomb was constructed in the 1920's and is situated in Chau Chu Mountain. As the name suggests, this tomb was dedicated for Khai Dinh, an emperor of Vietnam during the French colonial regime. The compound that houses the tomb of Khai Dinh is not as elaborate as the other tombs of the emperors before him, but Khai Dinh tomb is very special because of its unique design. The walls surrounding the tomb are laced with drawings of dragons and the tomb itself is guarded by 12 stone statues. Since Khai Dinh spent a lot of years in Europe, the architecture of his tomb shows European influences. Similar to Minh Mang's tomb, this compound is elevated and requires some 130 steps up to enter the compound.

● Tu Doc Tomb

Built in the middle of the 19th century for the third emperor of Nguyen Dynasty, the tomb of Tu Doc is the most elaborate tomb complex for any emperor in

Vietnam. Tu Doc was the longest reigning emperor in Vietnam and because of this he was able to build a very complex compound for his burial site. The site houses grand temples, a tomb and palaces built on a lake. Prior to the death of Tu Doc, this compound was used as his summer palace. It is truly the most beautiful tomb in the whole country.

● The Royal Citadel of Hue

Because of its impressive architecture and its miraculous preservation and despite the numerous wars that occurred in Hue in the past decades, the Royal Citadel or the Imperial Palace of Hue is a UNESCO Heritage Site. The Vietnamese government is currently restoring some structures that were heavily damaged but majority of the structures here are still standing strong.

The highlight of the entire compound is the citadel's intricately designed gateway. The citadel gateway arch acts as the entrance hall of the compound. It has three archway openings and all are clad with sculptures of famous cultural icons like dragons and flowers.

Inside the compound is the famous To Mieu Temple. This temple houses the portraits of 9 emperors who were deemed worthy because they served the country well. The temple is painted red with a touch of gold and green. Another building that is worth a visit is the three-tiered Hien Lam Pavillion. Do spend time by the pond and admire the lotus flowers floating on it.

You would need at least an hour to walk around the entire citadel, so it is really important to wear appropriate footwear, bring water and wear a cap or hat.

• Thien Mu Pagoda

This is probably your last stop if you book a group tour with any of the many budget travel agencies in Hue. With seven stories, the Thien Mu Pagoda is the tallest pagoda in Vietnam. It was an important structure during the ancient times because it's regarded as the icon of the citadel. The pagoda was built on top of a hill at the northern bank of Perfume River and can be seen from the citadel.

What to Eat

Hue is also a food destination. Unlike the Hanoi's and Saigon's tasty cuisine, Hue's menu mostly comprise of food rich in herbs and spices. With every bite of Hue's famous dishes, your mouth will always taste a festival of flavours.

Bun Bo

Pho is a soup that is very famous in Hanoi and Saigon, but another version of this clear noodle soup has evolved in Hue. Bun bo literally translates to vermicelli and beef. This soup uses a round version of rice vermicelli noodles cooked in a flavourful beef and pork stock with ginger, lemongrass, chilies, and other spices. This is served with thinly slices of beef, cubes of pork blood and shank bones. It is complemented with a plate of lime wedges, mung bean sprouts, spring onions, onion rings, chili paste, mint leaves and Vietnamese coriander.

You can have the best bowl of bun bo at the food kiosks in Dong Ba market or at one of the stalls along Nguyen Hue street.

Banh Beo

Another unique street food sold in Hue is banh beo. This food is meticulously prepared as it is like a local version of pizza with various toppings. Its size is only bigger than a poker chip. The crust is made from steamed rice cake, while the toppings can be pork cracklings, dried shrimps, shallots, spring onions and fresh herbs. There are five pieces in one order and each order is served with a unique Vietnamese dressing locally known as nuoc nam cham.

Banh Loc Tran

This is like an oversized steamed Chinese dumpling but instead of using ordinary flour, banh loc tran is made from tapioca flour. The dough will then be filled with chopped shrimps and ground beef and these dumplings will be boiled until the dough appears translucent. It will then be served with a heap of chopped spring onions or fried shallot strings and the versatile Vietnamese dressing, nuoc nam cham.

Nem Lui

You can consider nem lui as the Vietnamese kebab because this is made from ground beef or pork mixed with garlic and sugar and made into a kebab using lemongrass stalks. This "sausage" will be then grilled over charcoal. Nem lui is served with rice paper, which is used to wrap the barbeque sausages. Vegetables such as cucumber, lettuce, carrots and green papaya can be also be inserted in the wrap.

Chapter 14: Hoi An

Another historical region in Vietnam, Hoi An was once a major port during the ancient times. Hoi An is located at the eastern, central part of Vietnam. It faces the East Vietnam Sea that and is a strategic location for commerce and trade. Because it was once a major port, the streets of Hoi An are great evidences of the different influences and cultures infused by the Chinese and Malay traders. Similar to Hue, Hoi An also has a UNESCO Heritage Site that aims to preserve these old houses and buildings used during these ancient trades.

How to Get to Hoi An

By Air

There are daily flights from Hanoi and Ho Chi Minh City that take you to Da Nang. From Da Nang International Airport, you need to travel another 45 minutes by car to reach Hoi An. You can easily hire a taxi from the airport..

The most reliable airline that you should check first is Vietnam airlines but for a more budget fare you can check Jetstar.

By Train

There are daily local trains that depart from Hanoi and Ho Chi Minh City to Hoi An. Unlike traveling by plane, it will take you around 15 hours to get to Hoi An. Only book the newer and faster Reunification Express train for a more comfortable ride.

Where to Stay

Since you have travelled far and have already spent to reach Hoi An, you might as well spend at least one night to make all the efforts and expenses worth it. Hoi An is a coastal region so most of the hotels here are of resort-quality, offering scenic views of the sea.

Hai Au Hotel

Recently received a Traveller's Choice seal from TripAdvisor, Hai Au Hotel provides cheap accommodations for transient travellers who want to do a quick stop in Hoi An. Despite its cheap deals, the hotel promises to give its guests a personalized service. Guests always leave this hotel with satisfied smiles; therefore, they spread word of the excellent service of Hai Au.

The rooms include free breakfast and free internet access. It has a great location; guests can just walk to the beach or walk to the ancient city. It is a highly recommended budget hotel.

Hoi An Chic Hotel

This mid-range hotel has truly lived with its name. The chic design of the hotel mixes the contemporary with the traditional. It uses hardwood materials in a very artistic sense. Once you are in this hotel, you would not even think you are in a small place called Hoi An and will forget that just outside the hotel are rows of rice paddies. Each room is tastefully accentuated by small artsy elements – a small wooden frame with a picture of Buddha or a classic camera installed on a wooden plank. You wouldn't even imagine how these simple accents can become focal points of the room. The bathroom is another thing. When you step inside the bathroom, you will feel part of nature because it is not the ordinary tile-clad room.

Accommodations come with free breakfast, free internet access and free use of facilities like the swimming pool and shuttle service to the ancient city.

Anantara Resort

This sprawling resort offers the best view of the famous Thu Bon River and close access to Hoi An's anciety city. Anantara Resort has more to offer than just a simple trip to the ancient city. This hotel gives guests numerous choices of what to do in Hoi An. Whether cruising along the river or taking Vietnamese cooking classes, Anantara Resort will make sure that you get a first-hand experience of what Hoi An is really about. If you do not want to do anything, you can just take a comfortable seat facing the river and spend the afternoon reflecting while sipping coffee, tea or beer.

The hotel is complete with amenities such as swimming pools, spa and in-house travel agency. It also offers cooking classes, lantern-making classes and painting lessons. A night in the hotel's Deluxe Balcony includes free breakfast, internet access and access to the hotel's facilities.

Where to Go

Travellers usually just spend a day in Hoi An as a quick pit stop between their intended journey to Hanoi or Saigon. Since you only have a day, it is best to plan out your schedule so that you will get to touch base with the best sights to see in Hoi An. Start your day very early so that you can spend more time in and around Hoi An.

Custom Made Suits, Dresses, Shoes and Bag:

You might be wondering why this is listed first in your itinerary. It is because Hoi An is filled with around 400 tailors, dressmakers, shoes and bag makers that can make you a complete set of suit or dress in less than 5 hours. Since this is big in this area and since the price is very cheap, why not try collaborating with a local tailor or cobbler to make you your desired outfit or pair of shoes? Feedback of the finished products' quality varies from "not satisfied" to raving reviews but if you want to be assured of a quality output, ask your hotel receptionist. A name that usually surfaces when it comes to custom made suits and dresses is Anh (093 570 5655). Give her a ring and she will go to your hotel to get your measurements.

Bike / Free Tour:

Are you a bike aficionado? Then book a bike tour the night prior and see the very green countryside of Hoi An. This province is filled with rows upon rows of rice paddies and this view is breath of fresh air especially if all you see is a concrete jungle.

This tour is conducted by a group of Vietnamese college students who want to do Hoi An the great favour of educating tourists about its farming and fisher folk communities. These students give the tour for free; however, the tour itself will still incur you some expenses such as bike rentals, ferry ride, local community fee, insurance and transfers fee.

What will expect from this bike tour? You will get to experience the real living situation of the farmers and fishermen in Hoi An. You will get to interact with the youth as well. You can learn carpentry from the locals of Kim Bong Village. You can learn how to weave sleeping mats and how to make rice paper as well.

For more information, check out www.hoianfreetour.com

Ancient Town of Hoi An:

After exploring the outskirts of Hoi An, you should make a point to go right to this famous ancient town. As a UNESCO Heritage Site, this should be a priority in your itinerary. Within the ancient town, you will see a lot of well-preserved buildings that tell you the story of the old Hoi An. It will give a nostalgic feel once you step foot in this time machine. Enjoy your stroll while shopping for souvenirs as well.

Entering the ancient town requires a minimal fee, which goes to the restoration fund of the area. As soon as you pay your fee, you will receive five tickets which will allow you to enter five of the 21 beautiful structures within this ancient town.

Do not miss out in visit the enchanting bridges in this ancient town. During the ancient trading period in Hoi An, the Japanese built the first covered bridge to make Hoi An more accessible to their trade. From afar, this Japanese structure appears like a temple because of the intricate designs and the pink columns but once you get closer, you will realize that is built on a river. Crossing over the bridge is free so you do not get to waste your ticket. Do not think of entering the temple within the bridge because it is not worth it.

Do visit the Pedestrian Bridge over Thu Bon River as well. This bridge was not built during the ancient times, but it is worth a visit. Take a picture or two of this unique bridge. Crossing this bridge will cost you one ticket but it is worth it.

You can also visit the Assembly Hall of the Fujian Chinese Congregation. This hall has a temple within, dedicated to the goddess of the sea. This hall was really built for the Chinese congregation, but after years the hall was transformed into a temple for the goddess Thien Thau.

There are many other structures that you can visit within the ancient town. Once the sun sets, you will see a whole new Hoi An because of the numerous paper lanterns that are lit at night. The ambience of the place turns romantic and you will fall in love with the colours and the view of the river.

What to Eat / Where to Eat

Hoi An is definitely a food destination as well. It is comparable to Hue in terms of having a unique cuisine that dates back to the ancient times.

Banh Mi at Madam Khanh's:

Banh Mi in Hoi An is probably the best in the whole of Vietnam. Before you tour the ancient town, get yourself first a Banh Mi from Madam Khanh who is regarded as the Queen of Banh Mi in Hoi An. Everyone is just raving about her Banh Mi because her unique fillings. Just have a bite and you will forget your name. Madam Khanh's stall is located at 115 Tran Cao Van Street.

Seafood at Tuyet Seafood:

If you want to take a break from the view of the ancient city, then take a trip to An Bang Beach. Along the shore you will see Tuyet's Seafood Restaurant, which is one of the best in the area. A must try here is the seafood eggroll, steamed crabs, and tamarind shrimps. The service here is great as well. The waiters are always ready to help you crack open the crabs and even teach you how to get the meat off its shell.

Cao Lau Noodles at Canh Buom Trang:

This unique noodle dish is only available in Hoi An because here is where this particular kind of noodles are made. The best Cao Lau Noodles can be ordered at Canh Buom Trang, which is owned and operated by a Chinese family who has been living in Hoi An for generations. The noodles have a characteristic smoky taste and are served with slices of pork, fresh herbs, mung bean sprouts and some secret ingredients.

Chapter 15: Sapa

Located at the northwest region of Vietnam, Sapa is known for its scenic views of the mountains, layers upon layers of rice terraces and the many ethnic hill tribes that give colour to the view. Situated 1,500m above sea level, Sapa is regarded as the "Roof of Indochina." Sapa is the capital of the Lao Cai province and where the main markets are established. This laid back town is visited by many mountain climbers who want to climb the famous Hoang Lien Son Mountain.

How to Get to Sapa

Sapa is closer to the country's capital Hanoi and I strongly recommend getting there by train. Currently, there are three overnight Reunification Express sleeper trains that leave Hanoi in the evening and reach Sapa in the morning. It takes 9 hours to get there, so it is better to take the evening train and sleep so you do not feel the length of the ride. This train will not really bring you straight to Sapa. The train ride ends at the Lao Cai station and from there you can hire a private car or ride a shuttle bus up to Sapa. The roads leading to Sapa are winding and the local bus drivers usually drive recklessly so prepare for a dizzying ride. It is highly recommended to bring a barf bag just in case you will need it.

Where to Stay

● Sapa Stunning View Hotel

Located 100m away from the tourist area of Sapa, the Stunning View Hotel offers the best of view of Sapa at a very low price. You can stay here for a week and not even dent your budget. All tourist landmarks and destinations from this hotel are a mere 10 to 20-minute walk. This small boutique hotel only has 20 rooms, which makes the service personal and top-notch. Ask the hotel's receptionists for any queries about Sapa and they will be more than happy to assist you. The hotel also has an exclusive tour service provider that can arrange you a hiking trip or a trip to the indigenous people's market.

● Topas Ecolodge

If you feel like communing with nature and want to be surrounded by mountains, you can stay at Topas Ecolodge. This ecolodge is 45 minutes away from Sapa's famous tourist street, so all travellers who choose to stay here really intend to hike up a mountain. The owners of Topas believe in the principle of green living so all materials used for the lodge are recycled. Also, Topas Ecolodge follows principles that do not harm the environment around it. These principles come with some sacrifices such as conservation of electricity and water by not installing televisions in the bungalows, not building swimming pools, etc. The lodge also sometimes experiences power outage and water shortage during planting season. What is applauding about this lodge is the fact that they do not cover up any of these predicaments because they do not want their clients to be misled.

• Sapaheavenly

If you want to experience living and being entertained by an ethnic tribe Hmong local, then you better stay at Sapaheavenly. This home stay is owned by Dat and his wife and together they act as the managers, staff, housekeepers and chefs of Sapaheavenly. Dat is a trained chef who left the profession for his hiking love. He thought of converting his home to a home stay to welcome his hiking students. As a local and an experienced hiking guide, Dat will surely welcome you to his home with open arms and you are assured to have a delightful stay. To know more about their services, visit www.sapaheavenly.com.

What to Do in Sapa

Sapa is a true hiking destination. Every traveller who goes here intends to climb the magnificent mountains around Sapa. However, there are many other activities aside from hiking that Sapa can offer to those less adventurous. Here are some of the sights to see in Sapa:

Sapa's Main Square :

The main square of Sapa is a very spacious area where a lot of locals sell their ethnic products. Aside from mingling with the locals, you must also go inside the Holy Rosary Church, also known as the Stone Church, which is the focal point of the square.

Sapa Market:

If you have been around Vietnam, you might give this activity a pass thinking that all markets are one and the same, but Sapa Market is different. This market is a representation of the cultures of the myriad of ethnic tribes living on Sapa's hillside. Of course you will find local herbs, vegetables, livestock and poultry, but you can also find all the local handicrafts created by these tribesmen. Aside from the products sold, this is probably the only market that has vendors clad with colourful traditional ethnic clothing. Ready you cameras because this is such a colourful site.

The View of Sapa:

Some of Sapa's foreign guests do not even leave their hotels or homestays; instead, they just stay by the balcony while sipping coffee or drinking beer surrounded by the breath taking views. Sapa is one place where travellers can do a personal retreat and reflect about life, similar to what the character of Julia Roberts did at "Eat, Pray, Love". Sapa is a perfect sanctuary for those who want to rethink their lives and press their "reset" buttons.

Activities Around Sapa:

Again, Sapa is a hiking haven. You simply cannot go and not attempt to hike. Reaching Sapa is actually a hike in itself; although you can reach Sapa via shuttle bus or a private car, the fact that you are in Sapa means that you are 1,500m above sea level so what is another hundred meters of hike?

There are plenty of ethnic locals whose lives have improved due to the commerce brought by the foreign hiking communities that travel to Sapa. Instead of just farming, the locals now have a second job – hiking guides. They are the best guides of course because they know the place like the back of their hands.

Fansipan Peak:

If you really want to reach the real "Roof of the Indochina" then you have to climb and reach the peak of Fansipan or Phan Xi Pan. With a height of 3,143m, this is the tallest mountain in Vietnam. Unfortunately this peak is not for the faint of heart, nor for the unexperienced. You would need to get and pay for a permit from the National Park Office, which could be a dead end. For a more convenient but much expensive option, you can hire a private guide who offers solo and group hikes. It requires two days to reach the mountain's peak: the first day is a hike from Sapa to the high base camp, while the second day is a hike from the base camp to the peak and back to the base camp. Only experienced hikers must venture to Fansipan because unexperienced hikers can get altitude sickness due to the thinness of the oxygen.

Cat Cat Falls:

For a much easier trek, you can just follow the trail to the famous Cat Cat Falls. You do not even need to hire a guide because the trail is easy to follow. The trail to Cat Cat Falls starts right after the Cat Cat Hotel, towards the National Park, and goes down to the falls. You can choose to cross the river via a suspension bridge and then go up the steep path and finally hire a motorbike to bring you back to your hotel.

Chapter 16: Nha Trang

If Sapa is the best side trip destination from Hanoi, then Nha Trang is the best from Ho Chi Minh City. If Sapa offers the best view from its peak, Nha Trang offers the best panoramic views from its shores.

Nha Trang is a very popular tourist destination because of its wonderful stretch of beaches and dive spots. Every year, more and more transient travellers and backpackers visit Nha Trang as a side trip from Saigon or Hanoi. Since there is a tourist increase, Nha Trang opened its doors to international events like Miss Earth contests, as an avenue to showcase its natural beauty. Not only is Nha Trang gaining popularity amongst tourists, it has also gained a lot of interest from marine biologists. The place now has an oceanography institute where locals and foreigners can study the earth's hydrosphere and marine life.

How to Get to Nha Trang

As mentioned in the previous chapters, the Reunification Express Train is probably the best and cheapest way to get to Nha Trang from Saigon City. There are 400 kilometers between Saigon and Nha Trang, so it is best to leave Saigon at night, reaching Nha Trang early in the morning. Get the 4 person VIP Berth so that you can have a more comfortable bed for the 7-hour travel time. Remember to get the Reunification Express Train ticket because this is the newest, cleanest train in Vietnam. The other trains might not have the same facilities as this one.

Where to Stay

● Mia Resort

This is probably one of the best luxury resorts in Nha Trang. If you have come to splurge and really rest and relax with your friends or family, then this is the best resort for you. It offers a variety of accommodations — condo units, villas, and suites; all these accommodations showcase the best view of Nha Trang's coastline. Aside from excellent choices for accommodations, Mia Resort has a lot of activities and amenities exclusively for its guests. Some of these are an infinity pool, top-class spa, cooking classes, kid's club, scuba diving tours and classes, and many more.

● Dung Trinh Hotel

If you only plan to relax but still keep your budget on check, then you can book with Dung Trinh Hotel. This is probably the best budget hotel located at the heart of Nha Trang. Since it is in a central location, this means you rarely spend for transportation. You can easily walk to the market and to the beach from this hotel. It is truly worth it!

What to Do

Nha Trang is probably the one location in Vietnam that can satisfy all sorts of travellers. In Nha Trang, beach lovers, mountain hikers, history buffs, shopaholics and certified foodies can all travel together without having to argue on what activities to do. All activities that will and can satisfy a variety of travellers are here in Nha Trang.

Snorkel or Scuba Dive:

Do you want to have an underwater venture? Nha Trang has a multitude of dive shops that offer very cheap dive classes or dive tours for both local and foreign clients. Try to canvas around and find the best bargain before you confirm your booking. One of the more popular and more credible dive shops in Nha Trang is the Ocean 5 Dive. Look for Brad or Tiffany and arrange your diving lessons or tour with them. You will surely have a wonderful time looking at different marine species in Nha Trang.

Bao Dai Villas:

If you want to satisfy the inner mountain climber in you, then arrange for a hike to the Bao Dai Villas. This is a very easy climb, yet the view offered on the summit is fantastic. Aside from the panoramic view of Nha Trang, you will also learn a bit of history as you take a look at the old Bao Dai Villas. These villas are not converted into hotel units but before these villas were used as the official house of Vietnam's last emperor, Bao Dai. You can easily hire a cab to bring you to the foot of the hill and you can climb up from there.

Cho Dam Market:

Satisfy your shopping itch at Cho Dam Market. This market is an open air market that sells just about everything — clothes, knock-off bags and watches, fresh produce, street food and much more. A 5 minute taxi ride will take to one of the two markets in Nha Trang. When you find something nice, do not just buy it right away. Bargain, bargain, bargain! Since Nha Trang is flocked by tourists, some vendors have jacked up their prices so it's best to bargain to half or even a fourth of the original price that they're offering. Aside from shopping, do try some of Nha Trang's street food like Banh Mi and Pho.

Thap Ba Hot Springs:

This is a perfect activity after your train ride to Nha Trang. After that bumpy and somewhat cramped 7-hour ride, do proceed to Thap Ba Hot Springs in Ngoc Son Street and take a dip in their mineral pools. The water is real natural hot springs coming from the mountains and it is believed to heal illnesses and relax tired muscles.

Chapter 17: Other Must-See Places in Vietnam

There are a lot more places in Vietnam that are worth the visit. Most of these places are accessible by the Reunification Express Train.

Dalat or Da Lat

Dalat is the provincial capital of Lam Dong which is part of Vietnam's Central Highlands. Located north of Saigon City, Dalat can be accessed from Saigon by bus, plane or train. A bus ride to Dalat is almost 8 hours long, while the train ride is a little less than 7 hours. Dalat was one of the favourite places of the French during the colonial regime because of its unique climate and topography. Since Dalat is situated on a plateau, the weather here is cool and the vegetation is also unique. You can see a lot of pine trees surrounded Dalat, which really proves that the weather is cold and the topography is high.

Adventurers will truly love Dalat because of the many heart-racing, adrenaline-pumping activities that can be done. You can contact the famous Dalat Passion Tours and arrange a canyoning and rappelling tours with one famous guide named Gold. Rappel while going down a waterfall; it is a real wet and wild experience.

If you have a faint heart but still want to experience the uniqueness of Dalat, then you can do sightseeing activities and go to the Flower Park or take a look at the famous Thien Vuong Pagoda and Truc Lam Temple.

My Tho and Ben Tre

Just a few hours bus ride from Saigon City is the famous My Tho, the capital of Tien Giang Province. A lot of budget travel agencies in Saigon offer a day trip to this destination to show the tourists some of the local cottage industries as well as the famous floating market along the banks of the great Mekong River. A trip to My Tho will give you a first-hand experience of bargaining for fresh produce, while you are on a narrow boat and the vendors are as well.

A trip to My Tho is always partnered with a side trip to Ben Tre. At Ben Tre, tourists can learn about the traditional art of fruit candy making as well as the art of making rice wine.

Vung Tau

Another beach destination a lot closer to Ho Chi Minh City is Vung Tau. Accessible by ferry or by bus, Vung Tau is often flocked by locals who want to cool off from the intense heat of summer. It is not as nice as the beaches in Nha Trang; however, if you do not want to wait 8 hours just to reach paradise, then you would have to settle for this second best. Expect the place to be filled with people and tourists who are here to party or sunbathe.

Chapter 18: Vibrant Vietnam

Are you convinced enough to travel around Vietnam? Where can you find a place where the east meets the west? Where the heavens kiss the land? You can only find it here in Vietnam.

Traveling to Vietnam can be compared to a person's moods. You can travel low one day and then travel high the following day. Here in Vietnam, you can never have a monotonous feeling because everything is just spiced up by the people, food and sceneries – all of which are uniquely Vietnam.

It is highly recommended that you spend a minimum of 10 days to be able to explore the full length of our country, from the Northern tip to the Southern base. Don't you worry about the budget; everything and anything here in Vietnam is cheap from a Western standpoint.

Experience the unique culture and the distinct way of life here in Vietnam. Mingle with the locals to find out just how friendly and warm they are. Eat and drink the local cuisines to appreciate the history and the simplicity that it comes with it. Finally, walk on the paths that the locals traverse to fully identify with their past, understand their present and foresee their future.

Travel now to our vibrant place called Vietnam!

PS: Can I Ask You For A Special Favor?

Hopefully this guidebook has given you some ideas about what to do during your stay in Vietnam!!

We would like to ask you for a favor, would you be kind enough to leave a review for this book on Amazon? It'd be greatly appreciated!

Thanks a lot.

Preview of "Kuala Lumpur - By Locals"

We edit and publish travel guides from several cities in the world, all written by locals. When you plan your next destiny, please check on Amazon if we are covering that city already. If not, we will probably writing about it soon, please give us some time.

We would like to give you an advance of our Kuala Lumpur Guide, which is very special. Please take a look:

Chapter 1: Brief History Of Kuala Lumpur

Kuala Lumpur is the capital of Malaysia, a tropical country situated at the Southeast Asian region. Being the most populated city in Malaysia, it is home to many skyscrapers, numerous attractions, and several shopping malls. Despite the bustling ambience of the city, many do not know that Kuala Lumpur used to be a swampy, damp area bounded by rivers, which is very far from the city that we know today.

The country's capital was accidentally discovered by a group of Chinese men who were searching for Tin. These Chinese miners camped out near the Klang and Gombak rivers and started their quest for Tin. Lo and behold the swampy area turned out to be rich with this metal. This discovery attracted more miners from neighboring places who fought for the control over the precious metal. As expected, a civil war broke out between the Malays and the Chinese and destroyed Kuala Lumpur. This event pushed the British government to take action and create a new plan of moving the seat of government from Klang to Kuala Lumpur. This led to the formal announcement in 1896 that made Kuala Lumpur the capital of the Federal States of Malaysia.

Kuala Lumpur is a name given by the Chinese miners who camped out in the Klang and Gombak region. It meant "muddy confluence" which was directly related to the physical appearance of Kuala Lumpur's past topography. So Kuala Lumpur literally means the muddy area where the Klang and Gombak rivers meet. More than a hundred years from this accidental discovery of the Chinese miners, Kuala Lumpur is distant from being that old muddy place but still stays true to being a confluence where all cultures from around the globe meet.

Currently, Kuala Lumpur is one of the top 10 most visited cities in the world with almost 9 million tourists each year. The city takes pride of its unique ambience where the past and present unite. Here in Kuala Lumpur you can find state-of-the-art architectural structures in one street and old, nostalgic structures in the next. You can set foot in a high-end shopping mall and can traverse a vibrant street market. You can also taste different international cuisines yet still have that local touch. There are so much more that the Federal City of Kuala Lumpur can offer.

Chapter 2: Getting To Kuala Lumpur

By Air

Kuala Lumpur is one of the most accessible cities from all around the globe. Why then will it be part of the top

10 most visited places if it is not easily reached? Malaysia has three major airlines that can be your gateway to Kuala Lumpur. If you are coming from a nearby Asian country like India or Nepal, then your top 2 choices should be Malindo Air and AirAsia. However if you're flying from North America, Europe, or even Africa, then you can book with Malaysia Airlines. There are actually many airlines that service Kuala Lumpur so you can just simply check with your country's official airline.

Kuala Lumpur has two international airports – Kuala Lumpur International Airport 1 or KLIA1 and Kuala Lumpur International Airport 2 or KLIA2. KLIA1 serves as one of the busiest airport hubs in Southeast Asia. This airport services an average of 40,000,000 passengers per year either traveling to Malaysia or just laying over to connect to another destination. Despite the many passengers that land here, the airport's strict administrators make operations seem smooth and the atmosphere relaxed. The other terminal, KLIA2, serves as the landing port for international and local low cost carriers. It may serve passengers of budget airlines but this airport's stature appears grand and elegant. KLIA2 connects to a large shopping mall called Gateway which is filled with famous local and international boutiques, coffee shops, and restaurants. Visitors landing in either KLIA1 or KLIA2 will instantly feel the vibe of the city.

By Bus

Singapore is the closest country to Kuala Lumpur. Most of the tourists who visit Singapore also allot ample time to pass by here or even its outskirts. Taking the bus is one of the cheaper alternatives to reach Kuala Lumpur. There are more than 10 bus companies in Singapore that offer express transportation to KL. One way bus ticket to KL usually costs from US$22 to US$35 depending on the kind of bus you want to take. It is only an easy 5-hour journey from these two cities.

Travelers coming all the way from Vietnam, Cambodia, Myanmar, Laos, or Thailand can also make their way to Kuala Lumpur by bus. This mode of transportation is mostly ideal for the rustic backpackers who want to enjoy natural sceneries and to take in the many cultures of the different places they will visit. Of course traveling by bus from Vietnam or Thailand to KL may take more than 24 hours but the costs is less than half the price of airline tickets. So this cheaper alternative is for those who have a lot of free time but not a hefty budget.

Chapter 3: Transportation System Within Kuala Lumpur

From the Airport to the City Center

There is quite a long distance between the 2 international airports and Kuala Lumpur. Traveling to the city center may take an hour or so depending on the traffic situation. The good news is that Kuala Lumpur has a world-class transportation system in place. It is affordable and reasonable for travellers coming from all walks of life. Once you reach the airport, either KLIA1 or KLIA2, you can already feel the convenience because of the many transportation choices given to tourists.

The fastest way to reach the city center of Kuala Lumpur is via the express train known here as the KLIA

Ekspres. The platform of KLIA Ekspres train is accessible from within the airport premises. There are plenty of signs that will easily lead you to the train platform. If you are still confused, there are information desks in and around the airport and the airport's personnel can speak English fluently. The fare from the airport to KL Sentral station is around US$10 for adults and US$4 for children below 12 years old. If you are traveling on business and you want to reach your hotel the fastest way possible, then this should be your first choice. The only disadvantage of taking the express train is that you still need to transfer to a taxi, another train, or to a bus in order to get to your desired destination.

Although KLIA Ekpres is the fastest route to KL Sentral, it can end up being more expensive when you are traveling with friends or family. If you are more than 2 people traveling together, then your better option is take the budget or premium taxi services offered in the airport. The fare is fixed and can just be purchased from authorized taxi booths so there is no chance that you can get scammed. The budget taxi can accommodate around 2 to 3 passengers with small luggage while the premium can fit 3 to 4 passengers with small luggage. The average taxi fare from the airport to a destination within Kuala Lumpur's business or commercial district is US$25 which actually costs less than when you take the KLIA Ekpres. The advantage of the taking the taxi is that it will directly bring you to your desired destination; although it may take you an hour to reach your destination.

If you have a lot of time to spare plus you want to save up on your Ringgit, then you can take the third option which is the bus transfers. There is an Airport Coach Bus service that takes locals and tourists to and from the airport and KL Sentral. A one way ticket only costs US$3 and buses leave every 30 minutes from 5am to 12:30am the following day. So if you're coming in from a budget, red-eye flight you are assured that you have an available bus that can bring you to the city center.

Klang Valley Rail Transit

The main transport system in KL is the Klang Valley Transit system. This is a collection of 9 different train lines that service the city's residents as well as its visitors. These lines intersect in many points to give riders alternatives and options.

The first line or the blue line is known as the Seremban Line operated by the KTM Komuter. With 27 stations and over 153km in travel distance, Seremban Line services passengers going to and from Rawang and Sungai Gadut.

The second line or the red line is a popular line for tourists because of its stop, Batu Caves. This line is called the Port Klang line which is also operated by the KTM Komuter. This line services passengers going to and from Batu Caves and Port Klang. It has 23 stations and more than 45km of travel distance from the first station to the last.

The third line or the orange line is the Ampang Line. This line has 18 stations within its 15km route. It services passengers traveling to and from Sentul Timur and Ampang.

The fourth line or the brown line is the Sri Petaling Line which is operated by Rapid Rail. This line currently has 18 stops between Sentul Timur and Sri Petaling; however an 18-km expansion will add another 11 stops on this line that will eventually connect to the fifth line which is Kelana Jaya Line.

The fifth line or the pink line is known as the Kelana Jaya Line. This is another line that most tourists take to reach famous landmarks such as the Petronas Twin Towers, the KLCC Aquaria, the Trade Center, and many more. Operated my Rapid Rail, this line has 23 stops over a span of 29km. This line will soon be connected to the Sri Petaling Line to service more people and places.

The sixth and the seventh lines are the KLIA Ekspres and KLIA Transit respectively. These two lines have parallel routes however their difference is in the number of stops each route makes. The KLIA Ekspres is a straight journey from the airport to KL Sentral, while the KLIA Transit makes 3 stops before reaching KL Sentral. Despite the difference in the number of stops, both lines' fares to KL Sentral are the same.

The eighth line or the green line is very cute KL Monorail Line. This line has the shortest and smallest tram in KL. Plus unlike the other lines, the KL Monorail is elevated and runs over some of the city's major roads. The KL Monorail has 11 stations over a span of almost 9km. This line can bring you to the famous high-end shopping mall in KL, the Pavilion and to the cheapest electronics store, the Low Yat Plaza.

A ninth line is now under construction in Kuala Lumpur. This will be operated by Rapid Rail and is seen to be the most vital line in the entire Klang Valley Rail Transit system as it is projected to have 33 stations over a span of 51km. This line is expected to be finished and fully operational by 2017.

All of these lines converge in the center which is the KL Sentral Station. KL Sentral Station is the busiest station in Kuala Lumpur and the biggest railway station in Southeast Asia. The station itself has a myriad of small stores that sell clothes, food, and accessories among others. It also has a number of ticketing booths and ticketing machines that connect passengers to their next stations. KL Sentral also connects to bus ports that can take passengers to the inner commercial as well as residential districts in KL.

Taxis

Generally there are two kinds of taxi cabs or more locally known here as "teksi" roaming the main roads of Kuala Lumpur. These are the metered taxis, "bermeter" as we call it, which are red and white colored sedans and the executive taxis or "eksekutif" to us locals which are the blue colored mini-vans. The executive taxis have higher base fares than the metered ones and usually station outside big hotels. On the average, a 30-minute travel around the city will cost US$14 give or take.

The overall reputation of the taxi system here in KL has been tainted due to some abusive drivers who insist on not using the meter and overcharging passengers. This is mostly true for the red and white taxi cabs that drive around KL. The executive taxis maybe more expensive but the drivers are generally more polite. Before riding a taxi, make sure that the driver will use the meter, make sure that you both understand your destination, and make clear that you are paying in ringgit and not in dollars.

Bus

There are a handful of city buses going around the streets of KL linking the local passengers to the suburban areas within the Klang Valley. Most of our local public buses are operated by Rapid KL which is owned by the government and is also the main operator of Rapid Rail. This actually makes our daily commute easy because most Rapid Rail stations connect to a local bus stop as well.

Hop On – Hop Off

For the tourists who want to go around the city and see city's famous landmarks in one day without exerting much effort, there is a hop-on-hop-off city tour bus that roams around the city from 9:00am to 8:00pm. These double decker buses go through 22 stops and can bring tourists to over 40 landmarks. Air-conditioned with installed panoramic windows, KL's hop-on-hop-off buses are equipped with multi-lingual recorded guides which will help walk you through the city's famous landmarks. To even give tourists options, there are 24-hour and 48-hour unlimited passes which allow you to just hop on and off to any of the 22 stops. Each ticket costs around US$10 and US$18, respectively. Some of the famous landmarks covered by our city tour bus are KL Tower, Central Market, Petronas Twin Towers, Merdeka Square, and Lake Titiwangsa.

Made in the USA
San Bernardino, CA
08 March 2018